Up, Up,

Written by Tan

Illustrated by N

Short *u* and Long *u*	Consonant *Hh* /h/	Consonant *Xx* /x/
fun	hint	fix
mule	hit	
tube	hope	
up		

High-Frequency Words

blue	going	that	they	when
comes	new	there	too	yellow

1

I made a new kite.
It is yellow and blue.

There is no hint of wind yet.

The wind comes.
The new kite is going up.
I go up too!

I go for a fun ride.
I hope they do not hit me.

I can fix it.
I grab a mule.
That did not fix it.

I grab a tube.
That did not fix it.

When the wind stops, the kite stops.
I stop too.